Inventing Difficulty

Inventing Difficulty

poems by

Jessica Greenbaum

Silverfish Review Press

Copyright © 2000 by Silverfish Review Press.

Published by Silverfish Review Press
P.O. Box 3541
Eugene, OR 97403

ISBN: 1-878851-14-4

Cover painting *Gravity / The Way Things Are* © 1990 by Marcy Rosenblat. Cover design by Valerie Brewster, Scribe Typography.

Manufactured in the United States of America.

Acknowledgments

With thanks to the editors of the publications where these poems originally appeared, sometimes in slightly different forms:

Barnard Literary Magazine:	With Gulliver in Brooklyn
Boulevard:	Driving Friday Night
The Cream City Review:	a, b, c, d, e
Gulf Coast:	A Box of Clementines in the Maternity Ward We Want the Hurricane
The Kenyon Review:	"Blown-Away-Roof"
Luna:	"Civilization has a price."
The New Yorker:	After Rereading "Notes of a Native Son" Conversation About Life, After Life We Walked Out of the Hospital The Yellow Star that Goes with Me
Partisan Review:	Inventing Difficulty
Ploughshares:	Vassar's Orange Living Room
Prairie Schooner:	Back at the Cemetery Early Morning of an Argument, About When to Have Children The Sisyphus Report
Press:	The Don Quixote Jewelry Box
Salamander:	Grieving, I Came to Prospect Park Early in the Morning Three Poems Under the Spell of Miscarriage
The Seattle Review:	7:46
Seneca Review:	Outside La Roque-Gageac
Southwest Review:	Tolstoy's Snowball
The Texas Observer:	After Reading John Koethe's Poem, "In the Park" Brooklyn Aubade

Contents

Inventing Difficulty / 13

Part I

The Yellow Star that Goes with Me / 17
We Want the Hurricane / 18
With Gulliver in Brooklyn / 20
Brooklyn Aubade / 22
The Sisyphus Report / 25
After Reading John Koethe's Poem, "In the Park" / 27
7:46 / 28
Back at the Cemetery / 30

Part II

Tolstoy's Snowball / 35
Three Poems / 37
Vassar's Orange Living Room / 38
Grieving, I Came to Prospect Park Early in the Morning / 40
Driving Friday Night / 41
"Civilization has a price." / 43
The Don Quixote Jewelry Box / 45
a, b, c, d, e / 47

Part III

"Blown-Away-Roof" / 51
Early Morning of an Argument, in Spring, About When
    to Have Children / 55
After Rereading "Notes of a Native Son" / 56
Under the Spell of Miscarriage / 59
Outside La Roque-Gageac / 60
We Walked Out of the Hospital / 62
A Box of Clementines in the Maternity Ward / 65
Conversation About Life, After Life / 66

Notes / 71

Jed

One day they will go their separate ways and the fundamental question of whether the palm tree is a tree because it resembles a tree, or whether this passing shadow we cast on the ground is life because it resembles life, will remain unanswered.
　　　　　　　　　　　　　　—José Saramago,
　　　　　　　　　　　　　　The Year of the Death of Ricardo Reis

INVENTING DIFFICULTY

All music is what awakens from you
when you are reminded by the instruments
　　　—Walt Whitman, "A Song of the Occupations"

[Contemporary] American poetry lacks ideas.
　　　—John Haines, "The Hole in the Bucket"

You wouldn't say genius invented this world alone,
overthrowing difficulty to make our days waterwheels,
bucket turning bucket of light into evening,
and that underwater half rising to its tiara, Queen
Noon at the coronation. Perhaps a songwriter's

responsible for wind's attachment to leaves,
for the inseparable lyrics to earthly beauty we've memorized
before birth and come here with, already on our lips;
the way hearing "Prufrock" makes a slow groove in the brain,
then plays *you* hearing it again. Poets

make reunions, but what do we invent? *American poetry*
lacks ideas. I turn this thought over while testing
almond croissant around my city.... Usually deluxe and banal
simultaneously (a town my contemporaries *could* write into being),
today her housecoat familiarity

is undone by spring light, which loves her. If the world
came from stellar intercourse, two stars bathing together
and spinning us off, that's why we're spun off
in the morning, unmooring and drifting away, casting underwater
for the dream's biggest fish. Out in the glossy day,

sometimes the three dimensions detach, a circus family
jumping from each other's shoulders, and what's left are life-
echoing surfaces, glorified like the lake by a prostrate sun
whose back you ride, casting beneath the lid imagination
for why we're here. It's simple

inventing difficulty. With any five lines on the white page
of morning, I can fashion a skeleton of my world: a woman
fishing. The grasp of tedium and miracles keeps her from becoming
a let-go balloon, keeps her inventing both path
and obstacle toward a reunion with happiness.

Part I

THE YELLOW STAR THAT GOES WITH ME

Sometimes when I'm thirsty, I mean really dying of thirst
For five minutes
Sometimes when I board a train
Sometimes in December when I'm *absolutely freezing*

For five minutes
Sometimes when I take a shower
Sometimes in December when I'm *absolutely freezing*
Sometimes when I reach from steam to towel, when the bed has soft
    blue sheets

Sometimes when I take a shower
For twenty minutes, the white tiles dripping with water
Sometimes when I reach from steam to towel, when the bed has soft
    blue sheets
Sometimes when I split an apple, or when I'm hungry, painfully
    hungry

For twenty minutes, the white tiles dripping with water
As the train passes Chambers Street. We're all crammed in like laundry
Sometimes when I split an apple, or when I'm hungry, painfully
    hungry
For half an hour, sometimes when I'm on a train

As it passes Chambers Street. We're all crammed in like laundry
It's August. The only thing to breathe is everybody's stains
For half an hour. Sometimes when I'm on a train
Or just stand along the empty platform

It's August. The only thing to breathe is everybody's stains
Sometimes when I board a train
Or just stand along the empty platform—
Sometimes when I'm thirsty, I mean really dying of thirst

WE WANT THE HURRICANE

This dark morning finds us stocked with flashlight,
Batteries, bottled water, candles and the sly cache
Of hope: we want the hurricane, as the wealthy
Employ the luxury of change, but in this case
We want the hurricane, because, although we're stashed
In a big, book-lined apartment for the summer,
Only a natural disaster could offer relief from this climate
Of persistent agitation. *That summer we hardly slept. . . .*
It's not like that, we sleep better in this borrowed bed,
Falling off into separate, uninterrupted dreams,
Unlike the past year's fitfulness of being squashed
Into my twin-size, almost Hansel and Gretel, each head
Turning with the other, each evening full of seams
From surfacing in shallow sleep that barely covered our noses
As we lay, efficiently, on our backs. We sleep better here,
And when we wake up, we have to recover our bearings,
A parody of traveling, how we only do it
Within the neighborhood, packing our suitcases and garbage
Bags for the same city, where we are so lost.

Since everyone leaves this town in the summer,
We are left with their apartments, cars, typewriters,
Not all of which work simultaneously, as if
Some current runs between borrowed things and cannot
Let you have them all at once. We want the hurricane
Because it has been a summer of car trouble, plumbers
And broken typewriters (once three to a room!),
Of the toothy keys which just make worse our own
Inability to say goodbye. This summer we are at the mercy
Of machines, praying for the air conditioning and more
Prey to all the harshness of the town which rises
Then bears down, sun without a parasol,

Like the world was wool you had to wear beneath it,
Like the shopping strips and organized junk called
Intersections, like the modern amnesia, convenience,
Which substitutes the idea of something close
For the sought thing found, like the overwhelming banality
Could enter our blood streams directly, and we want
The hurricane to shut this city down.

WITH GULLIVER IN BROOKLYN

In the end I've had the life I own,
A massive pattern of imperfections, near misses,
Irreducible complications and debatable accomplishments
Which coerce each other, spiraling sideways,
So that I never know which way, if any,
I am advancing. It's the path a tumbling chair might make,
Or cat, grace tangled by a poison lizard
She once ate, who now walks as if three-
Legged. When friends call after years to tell me
Whom they're living with and where,
I mark their progress, the hoarse dispatcher
Hunched by her phone, imagining those kind ships,
Her friends, finding their bearings upon a point of air.
What once was common, becoming different,
Requires industry to patch raw space—cards,
Gifts, the ribboned act of faith that says *I'll follow,*
I'll follow you. Sometimes these six weeks
Seem like the last ones of my life, because he's here with me
As I replace the summer clothes with winter,
The black wools hanging in the closet
Like cocoons that I wish wouldn't hatch. The darkness
Comes on like that, from inside,
Although now we feel more like the heady orange trees
Than the early night they're steeped in.

Before he leaves (children
In another state) I try to memorize his shape (Gulliver,
Marooned in Williamsburg, across my bed),
To have him in darkness as I did in the light:
He has the optimism of bravery. His torso
Is a plain of truth. I rest there, as on a beach.
Once, poised above me in a stretch of pleasure,

He capsulized what misfortunes we'd come into—the writer's
Income a low flame beneath a jumbo pot of needs;
Religions rattling their importance until fatigue
Takes over; the wearing sense that we are losing
Whatever tiny assets we had gained
(Even the last umbrella, which stayed put in a cab that sped away
And left us freezing in rush hour rain);
But mostly, the vision of ourselves together,
Texan and New Yorker who chatter constantly like birds,
Walking down Atlantic Avenue to the Promenade or
Dancing to some good news years ago as if
We were built for happiness—and recalling
Our troubles since (from the crest we'd reached), said
This is to cover for all the bad luck—
Then came down hard
As if words or pleasure could make it up.

BROOKLYN AUBADE

The apartment's snake plants go up
In their placid, green flames,
While the sun, now hitting its stride
Over the unused Navy Yard, amasses
Lit properties from here
To the Trade Towers. The easy-to-catch
Industrial stacks flare first,
Their grey and black-lipped columns,
Buffed to the shine of military
Shoes, trip the first rays
And are taken. Next come the platform
Cranes, little white and red houses
On stilts over the water, their booms
Angled like early fishing rods
Caught in a net of light,
Then a Manhattan glass building
Whose green side turns to red
Or orange on a good morning,
Like a leaf through all its seasons
In an hour, or an otherwise listless mate
Whose chronic jealousy is incited
By the sun's daily overture
To Brooklyn.
Eventually, the Navy Yard's three-
Block-long, mildly blue hangar
(Was this for storing tankers?) is lit,
And the chorus of buildings behind it,
And the municipal stockyard in front—
The fire trucks, police vans and
Garbage trucks—all are collected.
Last comes the half-sunken pier
Where gulls circle and dip down

Like raised dust falling
And rising. The only action in the yard
Is the round of meditations
On what half exists. I remember
My last trip to Houston,
How we drove to the hotel,
Where the hotel used to be,
Where now stands the evacuated shell
Without towels, beds, lamps
Or curtains that a guest might draw
Against the relentless sun,
And we were never in those rooms
But we came almost every day
To the adjoining "Largest Outdoor
Hotel Pool." Padding in sandals,
Unbearably hot, squinting,
We watched them hoist
The building onto trucks,
The liquidating company's brochures
In the display windows where
Brooches used to be.
When we visited last month,
Recounting the tricks we played
To get in, and how we outlived
Those summers by sitting with our friends
And your children by the water,
We pushed up against the gate
And could just make out
The empty pool and the police
Sawhorses around it. Although
We have been forbidden
A certain continuation of the past

—Though I have forbidden this myself
By moving next to the Navy Yard—
The span and reach of your
Goodness moves with me,
Traveling every morning with your
Long strides, while gathering each tall
Memory, each reflective monument,
Any material we could use to fashion
A metropolis of water, metal,
Mercy, and the illuminating
Green flames of love.

THE SISYPHUS REPORT

I'd like to get away from the earth awhile
And then come back to it and begin over.
—Robert Frost, "Birches"

Summer's in its ditch. Shops close up and their owners turn
With the *Open* side of their signs, away from the street. Everyone,
It seems, is on brilliant vacations, little inventions
They're setting off over the globe. A sweaty haze hovers
From Mexico City or L.A., and those left to ride the subway
Gather that the sinner's afterlife will mean traveling
In this exhaust hose of a Manhattan-wide dryer. The garbage,
De rigueur, makes its splashy seasonal debut,
And everything trash-like about one's life
Starts stinking as well, since that's how garbage takes expression.
For instance, tonight, as my unsuccessful attempt at sleep
Stirs up the sediment of the past few weeks,
I see that the man I am trying to be close to
Is actually and irrevocably a maniac for autonomy,
That our plans are predicated on a fort of toothpicks
Which collapses when I bluster about like this, like
Tumbleweed through the dark apartment. Around 4 a.m.
I compare myself to those less fortunate, and guess
What, I come out tops, though it's a shabby kind of heap
I'm queen of. That's why I think: *vacation,*
For distance from the way my world presses on
All the wrong senses, and distance from the profound industry
Of art criticism that's every day more clever and deceiving.
I want relief from printed matter, because in these proportions
It's nauseating, the rate of obsolescence so dizzying,
It feels we're being constantly hurtled, but toward what?
I need a break from the endless, daily attempt
To feel a working part of satisfaction, from the mind bender
Of how to make these gracious, given parts add up. Tantalus and I
Share the burden of possibility; in that hope,

Futility is born. I have one handful of stones,
Bitter, unprocessable parts of myself.
Making fists so tight my veins arch through my skin,
I try to break them down. I don't have to push them
Over a peak; I have to push myself to a point
Where these emblems of self-hatred turn to dust.

AFTER READING JOHN KOETHE'S POEM, "IN THE PARK"

I am reminded of the question asked by my beneficent
Piano teacher: *"How are you measuring happiness?"*

The imagination wonders how the second half
Of life will look. When the mind clears away its first concerns,
Like a mountain table making room for higher
Forms of life, what will the mind
Want then?

As if the gull, black,
Then gone when it tilts its white side to the white sky,
Tips us off to the double life
Within us, and everything.

I am ready to reconcile all separations,
But I suspect this won't be possible until later,
When, as a natural reward for constant practice,
The world shows you its strings. Inside the belly of things,

You can see the gull. This key
Which makes a note and sends it off into a wave
To break inside us, this key is a good example

Of heaven on earth.

7:46

Because I took a job one town away
from where I grew up, every morning
I'm headed back, even the seats reversed
as the train moves against time,
against the nauseatingly hot wave
of arriving commuters. We take
their places, the maids and I, the bleach-
blonde forty-five-year-old always in the first car
(an easy stereotype from an alkie bar:
the dangling cigarette and surrounding
firemen, her face shiny as a scar), and now,
as every day, her mouth working on her breakfast
repulses me. Yesterday she bashed into me
entering the train, all menthol
and James Cain—and we head back,
out of the filial comfort of downtown Brooklyn
where our one skyscraper,
the Williamsburgh Savings Bank,
offers the hour from its pickle-shaped head.
Underneath it, below the slap
of feet against concrete, below the rose
and coffee shops and the grocer arranging
his pyramid of grapefruits,
we travel out to the botanical war-
against-disappointment that is waged
in my native suburban neighborhoods.
The blonde kicks a drooling coffee container my way
and our antipathy rolls into place;
she was also from these stops—from the family
who lived more poorly,
whose American flag waved
like a keep-out sign above their doorway. Long

Island: August light tamps down the space
between houses like snow, leaving a bright silence
most like the absence of sound.
Here sound seems warehoused
in the muscled homes, and even a pleasant yard
glimpsed from the window's moving frame—
tomatoes strewn on a glass table to ripen, a crooked lawn
chair—is chilled by the constant
boundaries, hedges, by a suspicion
caught, and dragging under our train,
that any reinforced house could double
as a fort of sticks, by the neighborhood's reminder
of what could not be found within the perimeter
of impatiens, the false note of the smoke
bush, and oversize, trumpeting-
to-no-one hibiscus.

BACK IN THE CEMETERY

where I took your *famous* picture,
      the oversize angel still weeps
            by the stone of Frau Louise Moeller, 54,

and her little Oscar, just one month.
      Finally, we are as much like stones as they,
         as the marbleized idea

of the eroded bouquet in the angel's hand,
      the original meanings we held for each other
         now mottled, smoothed,

devolved into nearly disinterested symbols,
      while the original, engraved memories
         don't erase (as we petition against

or for, depending). The first images
      still manage to hold the most sway—
         the actual feeling of that hot, bright afternoon,

my birthday, rising up through the past
      eleven years like a president making
         his way through a crowd; we were dizzy

from the morning's drive
      from the German lunch, from the whole Texas sun
         bearing down on this small branch of heaven,

from the mercurial, drunken
      initiation of the night before,
         and we napped beside the headstones

as if in a counter-production of *Our Town*.
      That's all. As the nervous half
          of our unbalanced affair,

I often stashed memory in the smallest gestures
      —to live beyond us—
          and they have. The uncovered emotion

of today's afternoon
      could have been for you, or equally
          for the kinder suitors who came later;

as year layered year,
      I did not achieve angelic grief—
          I was an aggregate mortal

and to each beau I felt I owed my life.
      Inadvertently, but with great relief
          I choose this place

to mourn all past courtships,
      and pair this week's tour
          through the Gulf Plains and Hill Country

with the surrounding low walls of layered rock:
      a monument between now and then. I am back
          in the cemetery where I once took your picture,

and am graciously lent this pencil
      from the very weathered man
          who mows the lawns around the graves.

Part II

TOLSTOY'S SNOWBALL

The day before spring, it finally snows.
Redefined, trees cast the opposite of shadows,
Their complex combs revealed again,
Adorned. *Blanketed,*
Yes, but nothing less than such a statement
Could describe, as snow does, each limb,
Branch, twig, each tree making its way
To detail, and today trees bespeak future detail
Since buds show through
Like bold words on the next page,
And snowy copses around Prospect Park
First outline what exists
Then burn with redness, like a visitor behind a veil.
New Year's Day we passed an elegant grey birch
Whose bare filigree suggested a diagram for smoke,
And now whatever burned itself away, going
Up in a diaphanous column,
Reinvents itself; the snowy branches
Extended toward my window could be an x-ray
Of extended conversation, of the inevitability
Action assumes, the motion of idea
And plot. (Ideogram for ongoingness,
The dendrite might as well be named
The human coat-of-arms.) I've been listening
To the unabridged *Anna Karenina*
On my hour's commute and with headphones
During my chores, unfaithful
To reading for the first time,
Lying with the long story while negotiating
The expressway, or choosing some grapes,
Or paying one fifty-six for them. Each word a snow-
Flake, I hear the author blanketing this world

With inclusive whiteness,
Laying bare the works of human nature
So that everywhere, even in the one
Short arm of the elm, we see a likeness.

THREE POEMS

Shane must have felt this way. You have to appreciate
A day whose brilliance reflects only absence.
The afternoon after, we lay down in thick light. (The disenfranchised

Own it.) A forgetful tide makes up, erases the bed.
You have to appreciate the local *chaise longue* fallen in oak boughs
The sun's inauguration of our shoulders and thighs, red begonias

As my witness. The tide rubs the shore's back, steals away.
The lawn chair with its knees up—a crumpled "N"—
Still suspended. I woke up in twilight, on the floor, dazed, late,

But you could appreciate it. Memory has a racket going with desire.
The whole house ransacked. Tibetan monks,
Comfortably tucked into themselves, hummed beneath the big tent

You have to appreciate domestic thieves. (Nothing renews
The dead more than the buckling absences and cryptograms they leave.)
—I dashed out. It was dusk, and very friendly. Beneath a tent

Of perfect ethics ethereal synchronization was held in suspension.
We found and lost each other, over time. You have
To appreciate the arbitrary shrines erected by devotion and the endless

Vibrations between the sacred, forgotten, and surviving present.

VASSAR'S ORANGE LIVING ROOM

A clear-cut wreck, I made the poet nervous
Asking what salvation writing could afford.
"You mean," she asked, more slowly than she thought,
"Like religion?" "Exactly," I said, knowing
She was a religious, solitary woman.
It was as though she guessed my real question:

"Can poetry keep one from the question,
'Why *this*? Why does sunlight make me nervous?
How can the solitary, still-housed woman
Live religiously enough to afford
Comforts she hasn't?'" Crippled and knowing
My real question, her adamant first thought:

"Poetry is not religion. It is a thought
We offer the house god, just the question
Faith asks our talent. A fair gift, knowing
How to order the world which makes us so nervous."
Well, I've embellished. Her answer afforded
A single division between the woman

And her savior. I was hoping one woman
Could do it all, but "Poetry," she thought
Aloud, "serves God." And Vassar could afford
Her year's dry spell because there was no question:
Sunlight is a loving sign. *I* was nervous,
Ill-balanced as a lawn chair, with no in-

Corporated god. Meanwhile, the knowing,
Resourceful, veritable folding woman
Sat opposite, withstanding her nervous
Disorder, far less collapsible, I thought,
Than her discrete body. It is a question
Of form, and hers, like a sonnet, affords

Grace from maelstrom; tailoring chaos affords
A corset of sorts, but better. Knowing
"Nuns Fret Not" (their tiny rooms) begs the question:
Can the less formal, free-praying woman
Forge a working trust with God? I once thought
The right hand could make the left less nervous,

But no more. Praying makes me nervous. Knowing
One woman lives in requited peace affords
This thought: the day is equal to the woman.

GRIEVING, I CAME TO PROSPECT PARK EARLY IN THE MORNING

and lay below the cross-thatched dome of two cherry trees
wreathed in blooms.

Dense as mattress stuffing, the pink clusters glowed beneath the sun's
impression.

Later, I saw the mesh as a million spherical puffs
skewered on a thousand thin brown sticks.

Perhaps the honeyed limbs had only to extend themselves
and shattered, drifting beauty
coalesced and stuck.

Back to back, I lay with our talented and possessive partner,
gravity.

The cherry cathedral pitches so transient a tent,
breeze was a parishioner.

Petals loosed from luxuriant globes floated, shimmered, and looped
through a last display, both formal and casual.
Each half the size and weight of daisy petals.

The individuals bruised and melted like snow. I stood up.

Rounding a bend in the park, I faced the erased circle
of the full moon in the blue sky.

Two boys, invisible at dusk behind pink curtains, shook the trees
to shivering. A peacock's thrill ran through them, then fear,
then arms let loose, as onlookers cheered,
everything held dear.

DRIVING FRIDAY NIGHT

The mind also travels. Through the darkness—
We have left later than planned
And are silent, dizzy, a little sick,
The week still running the body like a classroom
Taken over by its kids—

Rituals of travel get lost
In the haze of exhaustion and the mind's
Private racket. We are hypnotized, as by laundry,
By the questions tumbling over
And over,

By the possibility of seeing the moment they are answered.
As most do, this drive ends in stillness—
A huge, matched set with the mountain—
Punctuated by the long-gone city's analog
In stars,

And the invisibility of the trees, which we know have changed
Color, which we know are surrounding us
In a drama we are left all night to imagine.
We wake up
Through a hint of amnesia

And find we are caught between two monarch
Wings, the flashing yellow, orange and black
Of the woods, which stretches beyond (I'm afraid)
Our own imagination, to this question:
Did God consider what we would love

Or have we grown to love God's imagination
Because it is what we have? The cold-blooded
Salamander zig-zags through the leaves,
The lake's palette seems to hold
All paintings in one

Reflection,
While the sun's first self-image
Is quite humble, more like a glowing gumball
Then the monarch who has ordered
All these changes. Loving

You has been a lesson in aesthetic evolution,
One example of the way
We design the world through love,
Becoming native to what we find beautiful,
As it becomes native to us.

I am thinking of your face,
The skyline I see from the twentieth floor,
And these trees! They become their own definition
Of what we are meant for, and this planet
Becomes the right place.

"CIVILIZATION HAS A PRICE."

—Alexis de Tocqueville

When the wind turns their canoe sideways
You can see the line they cast like a spider's filament,
And where the sun's belly lets fall
Its white shadow, the shingled surface
Could be a miniature kingdom of white sails.
What if we did not have *dominion* as is said?
Under whose mastery would we build our boats?
Would they keep us from our routines of cruelty?
Voices, orphaned over the water, ride the wind and are at home.
Morning in the city, and any minute
My neighbor's kettle will hiss. The yards take their places
In the day's first light, and we are all back,
The mind released to conscious logic. Back too,
The illogic of suffering, the constant riddle of the fourteen-
Year-old starving boy—a bundle of kindling
With a face on the paper's front page—
And the political prisoner, even now, as greys turn to green
And laundry waves like a row of signal flags,
Even now she sits in the dark,
Violated more ways. One autumn day, reminiscent of the beginning
Of the world, we brought a picnic
To an apple orchard. The sun rode on the wind
and the grass shimmered in pleasure. A snake,
the living letter, crossed our path and disappeared.
Why were we given this moment of perfection
And the many more to come? How can any religion
Speak to one born to starve, or the one born to wait,
Or the one drained of pride, or the one born to have
Her clitoris sliced off? Who are the torturers?

43

What alphabet can ever spell their name?
They came from where, how, and how
Were we spared? Is it true we are all the same
Elements, just mixed differently? The estrangement
From what is monstrous or popular
Is always a surprise. And the narrow escape
To our own lives with their swarm of comforts, possibilities,
Their griefs as exceptions to the rule
(The prisoner still sits in the dark)
(And our own griefs run deep, even so)
What relationship has it to the seasons, turning
Over beneath us all?

THE DON QUIXOTE JEWELRY BOX

is the size of a playing card,
black lacquer, luminescent,
bearing a green, glowing rendition
of the Utopian on horseback
battling wind and windmill
under the full moon's light.
The wind shows itself in green
Van Gogh-like swirls,
gilded thinly where they're whorls,
as if this visionary also had a starry night
when traveling here from Spain,
then through the dark
Siberian taiga
where my far-flung friend
bought this as my wedding gift.
The moon is ripe, green in its shadows,
light with the light I see it with,
like the real one, while the windmill
tilts precariously on its pointy hill,
no match in this endless picture
for our advancing Knight of the Sad Countenance
who dons an antique, tasseled hat
and glinting shield,
whose lance looks fine enough
to paint the line of gold upon the green
swirls of wind, or sew his name
along their curves. His expression
is not the one we have come to know:
there is no derangement in his eyes
but a curious concern.
And neither is his horse
the dilapidated nag we might expect;

this Rozinante is delicate, but sure
to win, well-curried in his orange
cinch and saddle, his tapered hoofs
and styled jaw more reminiscent
of a fairy tale than this book
of well-meant folly. My friend,
 of finest caliber and ethics,
of honest passions pure
as natural wonders,
of intelligence whose depths
and sights we hoped he would
help us reach (and he did,
he took us with him
as far as we would go)
—my friend was lost,
with neither moon nor stars
illuminating his Alaskan
bush pilot's pre-dawn course.
Now all the powers of his gift—
the shining black, the gold
and green, the swirling wind, the lance,
the trusty steed, the windmill
and the hopeful shield, the *chance*
of redemption he gave life—
show themselves in this lacquered top.

Daniel Housberg 1957-1993

a, b, c, d, e

If the alphabet is the skeleton for our body
of experience, how great the burden on

a, already hunched over with all
it carries and anticipates, always

about to announce *b*,
whose bones, like the whale boat's

whale-shaped ones, bear stowaways,
then push a belly up to *c*,

who calls ahead with open mouth
then dashes into *echo*

like the archivist who snaps the shot
then blitzes for position

while the timer purrs, *c* hugging *b*
until a *d* appears

in the blurry snap. Then *c* and *d*,
in confidence discrete and doting, milk

Rilke's notion of betrothal.
Meanwhile, *e* messengers

an envelope through town,
private eye on a long trip,

finessing enemy lines like breeze
through barbed wire, and when

needing company (quite often its own),
doubles as an easy-mannered host,

offsetting the best in everyone,
a silent love letter in its grip.

Part III

"BLOWN-AWAY-ROOF"

The slight tambourine
of a hoe against rocks
accompanies the morning.
My neighbor's brown hat
dips and rises in the sun
as he clears off
the long rectangle of dirt
that is his on this earth.
His white gloves
emphasize the separateness
of hands from the body,
and when he takes them off
to pull a penknife
from his pocket
I am reminded how deft
an instrument
the fingers are.
From the third-floor window
where I spy on him
and on the grey kitten
who stalks his movements
from her side of the fence,
these open parcels of yards
(framed by see-through chain-link)
are like the convention
in Japanese painting
called "blown-away-roof."
In the illustrated *Tale of the Gengi*
for instance, we see into
a house from the top,
peering from above

what would be rafters
into what the characters
suppose is privacy.
From there we envy the beauty
of their rooms, the depth
of their desires. . . .
From here I see a cross-section
of what Brooklynites
might consider private:
the man now tying up
his bag of weeds;
a white moth bobbing high
and low beside pepper
plants in the adjacent yard;
the shadow of a plane
swagging over gardens
like a black pennant;
the kitten stepping through
ferns and staked tomatoes;
an unabashed bird scouring
the newly-turned dirt as
the nearby man stoops
and gathers
what long stems are left;
and now, as if in a primer,
the kitten following the moth
while a three-year-old girl,
from behind another fence,
clambers to grab the cat.
Once, after an afternoon
of relentless, hammer-like
barking from a neighbor's dog—

a buff-colored mutt
who whipped himself
into a fury as our images
ate bar-b-que
two yards away, and who then
scrambled to the top
of his dog-house roof
where he jumped, shook, and barked
with an endless urgency—
I shouted *SHUT UP!*
—*DON'T TELL HIM TO SHUT UP!*
shot back a fast reply,
HE'S ALLOWED TO BARK
IN HIS OWN YARD!
Today he is out of sight.
His grey shack sits
like a hermit's in tall grass.
Summer begins to set
its brand across our backs
and plant our shapes
across the earth.
Laundry is reeled out
with the flying images
of the family next door;
their winged shadows
dally in the zucchini rows
and move on.
Sometimes you and I lie down
in the middle of our yard.
It is a small circle
of grass. Bowered
by an overgrown mimosa,

it is more hidden
from me than the others.
But lying in its center
we are surrounded
by an order that has no
analog within our house:
flowers, vines, grasses and bushes
open toward each other
with a mixture of discretion
and collaboration.
You can only plan so far
before nature takes over.
I still wonder
what we look like.
Not down there, shoulder
to shoulder. Above
and beyond all that.

EARLY MORNING OF AN ARGUMENT, IN SPRING, ABOUT WHEN TO HAVE CHILDREN

Rain makes the air dark and the garden sumptuous—
Black earth showing off the separate greens.
The leaves of the miniature Japanese tree
Just opened in froth
Like the brim of green tea. One plant whose wide leaves
Overlap in the style of flattened pine cones
Is edged in white
And its two colors speak
To the green and white boughs hanging over the fence.
The bough's flowers are so small
They could be the phosphorescence on a wave crest:
Light from the friction of a body
Of water moving within itself.
Those hanks of tall grasses
Will soon buoy iris blooms. For now, the buds
(Sleeping, blue eyes of an Egyptian)
Are sleek, almond-shaped,
Half-cloistered by their stems. What is the opinion
Of the ferns,
Still bright green as a chameleon?

AFTER REREADING "NOTES OF A NATIVE SON"

I stood on the mattress,
stepped over my husband as he slept,
and made my way through the dark house,
picking up a beer, a cigarette
and a pack of matches in the kitchen.
I went down the dark stairs
to the open window, its plastic cover
crackling in the August breeze.
I pushed it aside (it made the sound
of a tent flap)
and stepped on the little wooden deck
which floats a story above the lawns.
The beer had been around for months,
and the cigarettes had been stowed
in the drawer for a year.
Everything tasted just as stale
as it should. The wind whistled
in the neck of the beer bottle,
the smoke wavered and stretched
like the cartoon image of ghosts,
and the midnight air of a Saturday night
felt colder than I thought it would.
I sat on a damp chair
and put my feet on the low table.
One light was on
in the apartment house opposite,
a window I have never seen lit.
A black man stood facing me,
laying out a pair of trousers
on his ironing board. After
smoothing them down, he picked up the iron
and began his work. He was studied

and intent at his task,
which he repeated, to my amazement,
garment after garment. The tool
of the iron, its palm facing me during repose
like the "Indian" greeting *Hau*,
seemed serene and historical,
like a printing press or loom,
and the man's industry was gorgeous
in silence, in the spotlit apartment window.
From the dark valley of backyards
I half expected his framed silhouette
would answer my questions,
the way the moon
responds to a graceless landscape,
but my husband and I—
we'd had an argument that kept me
from sleeping—
will still disagree in the morning.
I smoked and sipped my beer.
From the pendulous, dedicated
sweep of his arm, from its repetitions,
from the moment he took to assess his work
and move on, from his near
isolation, the rage
behind this composition—
myself and the man in Baldwin's wake,
ironing, and my husband, upstairs,
in sleep's even stitches—
gave way to observation;
the agitated sleeper is drawn outside
to blow smoke into the folds of wind
and consider the renowned essay

of mind and soul.
Then she's sent back in
to the bed she shares, to the cloth
curtain fluttering above
the cloth blanket,
to the essential work of marrying
acceptance and argument.

UNDER THE SPELL OF MISCARRIAGE

whatever I touched took on a lifelessness
of its own, recomposed like a sentence
to its letters or partisans to their hiding places.
The corn bread came out—a stone tablet—
and the soup, puffing, grew as bland
as its original pearly beans. Molecules spilled
their promise like the string of beads
I was trying to clasp; bonds broke so fast
it seemed no two entities could have rapport;
in the metropolis of my body all the friends
en route to assignations turned for home,
and outside it, even our speech fell bewitched—
ideas skidded to a halt before they could
be loved, and nothing we said generated a laugh
or begot more conversation. How I wanted
to talk up a storm, to spin a yarn, to harvest,
like the fair's cotton candy, a wand of stuff
from the kindness farmed in the plot between us
(because that is our defining nature).
A low bow to the one who forbids creation.
Now I see how powerful you are, and how neglected.

OUTSIDE LA ROQUE-GAGEAC

I came in the time of lilies and lilacs
Without a peck of encouragement from my courted world
Arriving in time for *coquelicot*, the poppies
Half freed and half waiting in their whiskery pods
And for *paquerettes*, a small blanket of them here
And there as if thrown in invitation because I was
Pregnant, often sick, in some phase of failing
Or falling, and so often setting myself down
In them—an airless ball through half its trail—
A Gulliver among Lilliputian daisies—
Wherever my momentum ended. I wished for a strong
Arm up, a promise that when I returned I could accomplish
Some portion of what I had set out to do
The way anyone wants to, and lying awake in the stone
Farmhouse I wondered how to remake myself
So not to become a woman lost in the lamps, pots
And linens of her home. Here the chimney tops
Kept watch like bodiless sentinels, their fireplace
Torsos erased in the hasty renovation,
And a pheasant couple wearing the colors
Of the countryside circled the shaggy pasture,
Jointing long stretches of night with their
Creaking, dry calls. If you were also up (because
We seemed to be traveling through time as well)
I opened my heart to you, as you did to me,
And we stayed awake chatting and laughing,
Even having small arguments absorbed like salt
In soup. Sometimes, with the bad luck of a flat
Tire, we came to an argument that still stranded us
After these five years, and then had to find
A solitary path back to sleep. But the thrill
Of getting to know you, again, more

Mirrored itself in our daily tours—not plodding
Through chateaux, but in the caves, their cold
Narrow walls pressing us to leave
Until the guide let fall her flashlight beam
On the Cro-Magnon hand print: an outline of a woman's
Prehistoric hello, or on the kneeling doe
(As the woman herself must have kneeled)
Being kissed by her reindeer mate, both drawn from stone
Pigment, ground and blown through a straw
In collaboration with the walls' warp flickering
In motion behind the torch flames, marking
The age with beauty and kindness, evidence
Of art before its own history recreating
Images from rocks and will and breath.

WE WALKED OUT OF THE HOSPITAL

                                on a mild early evening
in mid-December,
                the air barely dark, the winter
still lagging behind the oak leaves . . .

                 and we held her up to the sky

    (a fountain buoying a bubble).

My husband bought fifteen containers of Middle Eastern food
                then we holed up—the house
    a flea market of disorganization, the phone
                ringing even in dreams,
again
                          awake and asleep so often I
checked for my glasses before hitting the pillow . . .

            It soon became a winter of snow
            and record cold

for which, nearly alone, I was grateful
           each of us layered as if for a fall
                   —hoisting a handful of shirt
                  like an Elizabethan . . .

      Often I thought the wind woke me
                     to the sheet
      blankets
            my husband's new body
shutters, chattering like teeth
             then the evening's wide expanse

narrowed to a cry

noble in its isolation

and reached me as though I had been waiting
when truly, she woke me
(to all the rooms and all the bodies).

So I stepped into my suit
—laid out in the dark for that moment—
an outsize flannel print of cows
and we took
our places by the curtainless window

the imperfect chair, the unfinished room
inadvertently respectful of newness
and the sky's
inspection.
O mentholated moon
we are still on our own down here
lucky and...

Poor

poor archivists;
we committed to memory
the slogan of the brake
shop down the block

but lost the impress
of what was far more loved
and truly stopped us in our tracks.

One Thursday

—stuffed, suddenly, with heat—

winter ended like a long meal;
                        the baby looked us in the eye
            spring trees appeared like mist
            around the edges of the park

                        and the time of timelessness was over.

A BOX OF CLEMENTINES IN THE MATERNITY WARD

You couldn't sleep and you cried
unless I nursed you while I walked
around the room. On the oval table
in their small wooden crate
sat the clementines, packed neatly
and glowing like embers
beneath their red netting. Rounding
the dark room, singing a song
that came with you and is lost
with those early days (half of life,
my love, is disappearance) I stopped
at the table and peeled one clementine
every few laps, the skin falling
off the globe with completion and ease,
a yellowed veil barely clinging,
the little smoke rising to your initiating
dream, the whole fruit punctuating
my thirst and hunger. My body
was an enormous land you just left,
my belly so soft after your departure
it seemed to ripple like a lake.
Into that darkness
dropped the clementines,
both you and I lifting to our lips
something we tasted
for the first time, in an orbit we followed
without haste or destination.

CONVERSATION ABOUT LIFE, AFTER LIFE

I stretched out against the sky (as you may have done)
and tried squaring my outline with the many points of stars.
My pattern fit the constellations in a general way, like fingers
to a mitten. I cut the scraps created by the disparity
and kept them in a bag beneath the bed. I had hoped to fashion
a *chapeau* or vest, and appear as my true self when time allowed.
What was I thinking? I have never been able to sew!
Spring, summer, autumn, winter. . . . Each year passed like four
wheels carrying a covered wagon. Once, eating a mango
over the sink, I remembered an unbelievably satisfying
conversationalist—we managed every morsel off the bone
with progressively more blunt, more accurate responses, out-
doing each other in a spiral of pleasurable honesty that bribed
conversation beyond and beyond, to its furthest possible
ending place. With each admission, our green canoes went over
another waterfall, coursing closer to each others' hearts.
Which we found, truthfully. They were calm and beautiful
like mountain lakes addressing and reflecting the sky
in endless conversation. Our perfect outlines lay on their skin.

NOTES

"The Yellow Star that Goes with Me": The title is after the first line of Delmore Schwartz' poem, "The Heavy Bear."

"We Want the Hurricane": "That summer we hardly slept" is from a poem by Cleopatra Mathis.

"Vassar's Orange Living Room": "Nuns Fret Not" is an abbreviation of the title of William Wordsworth's sonnet "Nuns Fret Not at Their Convent's Narrow Room."

These poems carry dedications:

"Inventing Difficulty" to Stephen Ackerman
"The Yellow Star that Goes with Me" to Gloria and Lowell Greenbaum
"After Reading John Koethe's Poem, 'In the Park'" to Patricia Moger
"We Want the Hurricane" to David Theis
"7:46" to Matt and Dan Greenbaum
"Tolstoy's Snowball" to my former colleagues at *Choice Magazine Listening*, a free periodical-on-tape for people who are visually impaired. (516) 883-8280
"Vassar's Orange Living Room" to the memory of Vassar Miller
"Grieving, I Came to Prospect Park Early in the Morning" to the memory of Frank Crewdson
"Civilization has a price." to Miriam Ancis
"The Don Quixote Jewelry Box" to the memory of Daniel Housberg
"*a, b, c, d, e*" to Rose Weil
"Outside La Roque-Gageac" to Jed Marcus
"We Walked Out of the Hospital" to Isabel Daniela Marcus
"A Box of Clementines in the Maternity Ward" to Rebecca Rose Marcus
"Conversation About Life, After Life" to Vicki Ward

Thanks and love, old timers!
Susan Biskaborn, John Fading, Dorothy Field, Ramie Friedman,
Karen Gruebel, Robert Held, David Kaplan, Kathy and Karl Kilian,
Jamie Kitman, Louise Kramer, Charlene and George Shepard, Jonathan Siegel,
Regina Stone, Carolyn Vaughan, Lee Winder, Bill Zavatsky.
And to Rodger Moody, Ann Townsend
and Marcy Rosenblat